SERMON OUTLINES

on

Christ's Death, Resurrection, and Return

The Bryant Sermon Outline Series

SERMON OUTLINES

on

Christ's Death, Resurrection, and Return

compiled by
Al Bryant

kregel
PUBLICATIONS

Grand Rapids, MI 49501

Sermon Outlines on Christ's Death, Resurrection, and Return
compiled by Al Bryant

© 1998 by Kregel Publications

Published by Kregel Publications, a division of Kregel, Inc., P.O. Box 2607, Grand Rapids, MI 49501. Kregel Publications provides trusted, biblical publications for Christian growth and service. Your comments and suggestions are valued.

For more information about Kregel Publications, visit our web site at: www.kregel.com

Cover design: Frank Gutbrod

Library of Congress Cataloging-in-Publication
Sermon outlines on Christ's death, resurrection, and return / compiled by Al Bryant.
        p.   cm.
1. Jesus Christ—Crucifixion—Sermons—Outlines, syllabi, etc. 2. Jesus Christ—Resurrection—Sermons—Outlines, syllabi, etc. 3. Second Advent—Sermons—Outlines, syllabi, etc. I. Bryant, Al.
BT450.S37   1998   98-16988
232.96—dc21

ISBN 0-8254-2052-0

1 2 3 4 5 / 04 03 02 01 00

Printed in the United States of America

CONTENTS

PREFACE

Since there is already a book titled *Sermon Outlines on the Life of Christ* in this series, it was felt that a companion compilation on His death, resurrection, and return would be helpful.

We have tried to arrange these outlines in logical fashion under these three headings, but you may discover some overlapping or even disagree with some of the placement. We hope, however, that this collection will prove provocative and helpful for those who choose to deal with these challenging subjects in their preaching program.

Al Bryant

The poems in this compilation are used by permission and taken from *Sourcebook of Poetry,* published in 1992 by Kregel Publications. The hymn lyrics are in public domain.

SCRIPTURE INDEX

CHRIST'S ATONEMENT

The life of the flesh is in the blood: and I have given it to you upon the altar to make an atonement for your souls: for it is the blood that maketh an atonement for the soul (Lev. 17:11).

Sir Walter Scott makes one of his characters, Old Mortality, to be occupied in rechiseling the inscriptions on the tombstones of the Covenanters. Annually the old man visited the graves of the men who had laid down their lives for the sake of Christ and the covenant, and removed the moss and dirt that might have gathered on their monuments. We may do something similar with the chisel of the pen in reproducing those epitaphs that speak of the "unseen things."

In Bunhill Fields cemetery there is the following epitaph on the tomb of an infant: "In memory of Westfield Lilley, son of Westfield and Sarah Lilley, who died June 2, 1798, aged one year and ten months.

"Bold Infidelity, turn pale and die,
Under this stone an *Infant's* ashes lie.
Say—Is it *Lost* or *Saved?*
If Death's by *sin,* it sinned, for it lies here;
If heaven's by *works,* in Heaven it can't appear.
Ah, reason, how deprav'd!
Revere the Bible! (sacred page) the *knot's unty'd;*
It *died,* through Adam's *sin;* it *lives,* for Jesus died."

"Jesus died!" In the fact of Christ's atonement, as may be found in the following Scriptures, we find

The **antidote** for sin's ill (Rom. 5:8).
The **severance** from sin's authority (Rom. 6:10–11).
The **remover** of sin's condemnation (Rom. 8:34).
The **motive** for Christly action (Rom. 14:15).
The **separator** from self's aggrandizement (2 Cor. 5:14–16 RV),
And the **promise** of coming glory (1 Thess. 4:14; 5:10).

Christ's atonement is the expression of God's love in dealing with sin, and it is the extinguishing power to put it out. The fire of heaven consumes the flame of hell.

F. E. Marsh

9

CHRIST'S DEATH

We do well to remember Him who died on our account, for that death is:

1. The **basis** of faith's confidence (Rom. 4:25).

2. The **spring** of love's service (2 Cor. 5:14).

3. The **window** of hope's expectation (1 Thess. 4:14).

4. The **joy** of reconciliation's blessing (Rom. 5:11).

5. The **motive** of affection's regard (1 John 16).

6. The **soul** of the believer's praise (Rev. 1:5).

7. The **theme** of the Gospel's witness (1 Cor. 15:3–4).

F. E. Marsh

CHRIST'S DEATH FORETOLD AND EXPLAINED

1. It was predicted He would **die** (Isa. 53:5).

2. The **manner** of His death was foretold (Ps. 22:16).

3. He **said** He would die (John 10:18).

4. He **showed** the love of God in dying (Rom. 5:8).

5. He died for our **sins** (Gal. 1:4).

6. He died to **destroy** the Devil's works (1 John 3:8).

7. He died that we might **live** to Him (2 Cor. 5:14–15).

The determination of His will is seen in His "flint" face of purpose (Isa. 1:7), and in that He set His face to go to Jerusalem (Luke 9:51, 53), and He was not satisfied until He could say "accomplished." The word rendered in John 19:30, "It is finished," would be better given "accomplished."

F. E. Marsh

CHRIST'S DEATH—EIGHT QUESTIONS

1. **For whom did Christ die?** Christ is said to have died for "sinners" and for the "ungodly," and that God's "enemies" are reconciled to Him by the death of His Son (Rom. 5:6, 8, 10).

2. **For what did He die?** "Our sins." "Christ died for our sins according to the scriptures" (l Cor. 15:3).

3. **Why did Christ come into the world?** To "put away sin by the sacrifice of himself" (Heb. 9:26). "He was manifested to take away our sins" (1 John 3:5).

4. **Did God have anything to do with that death for sin?** He made "his soul an offering for sin" (Isa. 53:10). "He . . . made him to be sin for us" (2 Cor. 5:21). "God sending his own Son . . . [by a sacrifice] for sin, condemned sin in the flesh" (Rom. 8:3, mg).

5. **Did Christ die willingly?** "[He] gave himself for our sins" (Gal. 1:4).

6. **What did He do with our sins?** "He bare the sin of many" (Isa. 53:12). "Offered to bear the sins of many" (Heb. 9:28).

7. **Where did He bear our sins?** "In his own body on the tree" (1 Peter 2:24).

8. **Is it necessary for Him to repeat the act?** "Christ died for sins once" (1 Peter 3:18 RV, mg). Offering of the body of Jesus Christ once for all (Heb. 10:12).

F. E. Marsh

THE PLACE CALLED CALVARY
(GOOD FRIDAY)

The place . . . called Calvary (Luke 23:33).

A magic spell rests over some scenes and places. One's youthful home. Places of historic interest. Bible scenes for which we cherish a deep religious regard. Let us draw near this divinely honored place; the place where, be it said with reverence, we see Deity in conflict; "the place . . . called Calvary."

I. It Was the Place of Unparalleled Suffering.
A. No alleviating circumstances.

B. No softening of anguish.

C. The darkened heavens and the rent earth gave tokens of sympathy with the suffering Savior.

II. It Was the Place of Singular Phenomena.
A. Darkness.

B. Earth and sky put on their mourning clothes.

III. It Was the Place of the Most Momentous of All Achievements.
A. Here was the mightiest moral transaction.

B. On the brow of Calvary was the price laid down for a lost world.

IV. But, Also, Calvary Was the Place of Glorious Triumph.
A. Christ met stern justice, and silenced her demand.

B. He bridged the chasm between heaven and earth, and opened the way to glory.

V. It Was the Place of Pardoning Mercy.
In the very agonies of death He absolved the thief and took him to the courts above as a trophy of victory of redeeming love.

VI. It Was the Place of Deep Devotion and Ardent Affection!
A. "Now there stood by the cross" (John 19:25 27).

B. May you cherish like faithful affection toward the Savior.

Selected

"BEHOLD THE MAN!"
(GOOD FRIDAY)

Behold the man! (John 19:5).

For our Good Friday meditation.

I.   The Feelings with Which These Words Were and May Be Uttered.
A. Of pity.
B. In mockery.
C. In faith.
D. In admiration.

II. Let Us by Faith Behold the Christ of Good Friday.
A. Behold the Man of dignity!
B. Behold the Man of humility.
C. Behold the Man of purity.
D. Behold the Man of suffering.
E. Behold the Man of glory.

Selected

THE DEATH OF JESUS
(GOOD FRIDAY)

Where they crucified him, and two others with him, on either side one, and Jesus in the midst (John 19:18).

1.   The Awe with That It Fills Us.

2.   The Grief That It Calls Forth.

3.   The Repentance That It Preaches.

4.   The Comfort That It Gives.

Selected

THE LIFTING POWER OF CHRIST

The gospel . . . is the power of God (Rom. 1:16).

It is said that once a skilled artisan, in the employ of an Oriental king, had become almost useless at his daily tasks. His hand had lost its cunning, and the work was marred by constant failure. The king sent for him and asked him what had caused the surprising change.

"Ah," he said, "it is my heart that makes my hand unsteady. I am under an awful cloud of calamity and discouragement. I am hopelessly in debt, and my family is to be sold as slaves. I can think of nothing else from morning to night, and as I try to polish the jewels and cut the facets in the diamonds, my hand trembles and my fingers forget their wonted skill."

The king smiled and said: "Is that all? Your debt shall be paid, your family saved, and your cares dispelled. You may take the word of your king and go to work again with a free and fearless heart." That was done, and never was work so skillfully done, never were such carvings and cunning devices in precious gems as the hand of this happy artisan devised when set at liberty from his fears and burdens.

The king's grace made a new man of the artisan.

1. The power of **Christ's love** will lift us above hate and cause us to love Him (1 John 4:19).

2. The power of **Christ's joy** will banish the bane of misery and gladden us with its song (John 15:11).

3. The power of **Christ's peace** will turn out grinding care and fill us with its own tranquillity (John 14:27).

4. The power of **Christ's grace** will stiffen the muscles of our spiritual nature and make us of sterling worth (2 Tim. 2:1).

5. The power of **Christ's presence** will keep away all fear and sustain us in every emergency (Isa. 41:10).

6. The power of **Christ's armor** will shield us in every assault of the enemy as we are strong in Him (Eph. 6:10, 11).

7. The power of **Christ's beauty** will so entrance and satisfy that we shall not be distracted from Him (Song 5:16).

To deny self we need a greater power than self. Christ Himself is the only one who can dethrone and deny self.

F. E. Marsh

THE POWER OF THE GOSPEL OF CHRIST

The gospel of Christ . . . is the power of God unto salvation
(Rom. 1:16).

Griffith John says, "The great need of China today is vital religion, not a religion that *men can make great, but a religion that can make men great.* The Chinese need a heavenly principle that shall infuse a new moral and spiritual life into the nation, a mighty power that shall transform them in their inmost being, a Divine inspiration that shall create within their breasts aspirations after holiness and immortality. In other words, what they need is *the Gospel of Jesus Christ.* Apart from Christianity, I can see no hope for China. There is no power in the religious systems of China to develop a holy character, a true manhood. China cannot advance in the path of true progress without a complete change in the religious life of the nation. It is Christ alone who can lead in the glorious dawn of the Chinese Renaissance, the new birth of a mighty nation to liberty, and righteousness, and ever-expanding civilization. Feeling this to be true in our heart of hearts, we, the missionaries, have come to China to 'preach Christ . . . unto [some] a stumbling block, and unto [others] foolishness; but unto them which are called . . . Christ the power of God, and the wisdom of God'" (1 Cor. 1:23–24).

The Gospel has:

1. **Power to quicken** those dead in sins (1 Cor. 4:15).

2. **Power to enlighten** the mind darkened by unbelief (2 Cor. 4:4).

3. **Power to save** from the thralldom of iniquity (Eph. 1:13).

4. **Power to protect** against the assaults of the enemy (Eph. 6:15).

5. **Power to brighten** the future, so that the horizon is lit up with coming glory (Col. 1:23).

6. **Power to bless** the saint in the necessity of his experience (Rom. 15:29).

7. **Power to unite** believers in fellowship with Christ (Eph. 3:6).

There is no need of man that the nature of God cannot meet.

F. E. Marsh

CROSS'S POWER TO LIFT UP

Christ crucified . . . the power of God (1 Cor. 1:23–24).

"Look up" and "lift up" were the words above and beneath a cross in a glass stained window in a church in the Kentucky town of Louisville. The cross of Christ's atoning death does indeed tell us to look up and find in Him who died for us the canceling of the sinful past, the bringing of untold blessing in the present, and the making known of unparalleled glory for the future. But the cross, as the expression of what Christ has done for us, lifts us, as Matheson expresses it,

O Cross, that liftest up mine head.

The cross of Christ's atoning, as we look to Him who died there, lifts from:

1. **Slavery to Self.**
   "He died for all, that they which live should not . . . live unto themselves" (2 Cor. 5:15).

2. **The Trials of the World.**
   "The cross of our Lord Jesus Christ, by whom the world is crucified unto me, and I unto the world" (Gal. 6:14).

3. **The Tyranny of Sin.**
   "He died unto sin once. . . . Likewise reckon ye also yourselves to be dead indeed unto sin" (Rom. 6:10–11).

4. **The Old Man of Habit.**
   "Knowing this, that our old man is crucified with him" (Rom. 6:6).

5. **The Self of Sinful Self.**
   "I am crucified with Christ" (Gal. 2:20).

6. **The Lusts and Affections of the Flesh.**
   "They that are Christ's have crucified the flesh with the affections and lusts" (Gal. 5:24).

7. **The Works of the Devil.**
   "The Son of God was manifested, that he might destroy the works of the devil" (1 John 3:8).

F. E. Marsh

CROSS ENDURED:
OR A CROSS, A HEART, AND A ROSE

Jesus . . . who for the joy set before him endured the cross
(Heb. 12:2 NIV).

"I took for the symbol of my theology a seal on which I had engraven a Cross, with a Heart in its center. The Cross is black, to indicate the sorrows, even to death, through which the Christian must pass. But the Heart preserves its natural color, for the Cross does not extinguish nature—it does not kill, but gives life. The Heart is placed in the midst of a White Rose, which signifies the joy, peace, and consolation that faith brings. But the Rose is white and not red, because it is not the joy and peace of the world, but that of the Spirit." So writes one who saw beyond the symbols into the realities.

1. **Sufficient Grace** was found through the hurting thorn, as Paul experienced (2 Cor. 12:9).

2. **The Palace Was Reached** through the experience of the prison, as Joseph knew (Ps. 105:18–22).

3. The **Position of Leader** was entrusted to Moses because he had qualified in the wilderness of adversity (Exod. 3:1–10).

4. The **Skill of Accuracy** was learned by David when he overcame the lion and the bear; hence, he triumphed over the giant (1 Sam. 17:35–37).

5. The **Unfolding of the Future** was made known to John when he was banished to the Isle of Patmos (Rev. 1:9–20).

6. The **Companionship of the Lord** was enjoyed by the three Hebrews when in the fiery furnace (Dan. 3:24–30).

7. The Lord's **Delivering Power** was felt when Daniel was in the lions' den (Dan. 6:16–28).

F. E. Marsh

CROSS FORGOTTEN

The cross (John 19:19).

Rev. W. H. Armstrong, when speaking at a Wesleyan Conference in England of the influence of the early Methodist preachers and those of today, said, "He ventured to think the reason for this was, that in emphasizing the social implications of the Christian Gospel they had forgotten the Cross, which was the only effective dynamic of social service." The dynamic of the Cross is seen if we, having recognized its objective work (1 Cor. 15:3–4), ponder its subjective influence.

1. The Cross is the **death** of sin (Rom. 6:10–11).

2. The **slayer** of self (Gal. 2:20).

3. The **separator** from the world (Gal. 6:14).

4. The **begetter** of love to others (1 John 3:16).

5. The **soul** of holiness (Heb. 13:12, 20–21).

6. The **incentive** to sacrifice (Matt. 10:26–28).

7. The **mainspring** of service (2 Cor. 5:14).

8. The **music** of worship (Rev. 5:9–10).

9. The **hope** of the future (1 Thess. 4:13–14).

F. E. Marsh

In the cross of Christ I glory,
Tow'ring o'er the wrecks of time;
All the light of sacred story
Gathers round its head sublime.

When the woes of life o'er take me,
Hopes deceive and fears annoy,
Never shall the cross forsake me:
Lo! it glows with peace and joy.

When the sun of bliss is beaming
Light and love upon my way,
From the cross the radiance streaming
Adds more luster to the day.

Bane and blessing, pain and pleasure,
By the cross are sanctified;
Peace is there that knows no measure,
Joys that thru all time abide.

John Bowring

CHRIST'S BLOOD OF BLESSING

The blood of Jesus Christ his Son cleanseth us from all sin (1 John 1:7).

In the autobiography of the martyred James Chalmers, he recounts what gave him peace. He says: "I was pierced through and through with conviction of sin, and felt lost beyond all hope of salvation. Mr. Meikle came to my help, and led me kindly to promises and to light; and, as he quoted 'The blood of Jesus Christ his Son cleanseth us from all sin,' I felt that this salvation was possible for me, and some gladness came to my heart. After a time light increased, and I felt that God was speaking to me in His Word, and I believed unto salvation."

What a number have found, in the statement of fact that the blood of Christ cleanses from sin, a furnisher of blessing. Verily His atoning blood is:

1. A sin-remover (Heb. 9:26).

2. A conscience-healer (Heb. 10:1–4).

3. A victory-provider (Rev. 12:11).

4. A blessing-procurer (2 Cor. 10:16).

5. A sin-killer (1 Peter 1:18–19 RV).

6. A self-displacer (Gal. 2:20).

7. A world-separator (Heb. 13:12).

8. A love-inspirer (2 Cor. 5:14–15).

To be cleansed by Christ means more than to have the blemishes removed from the face of the life, it means the purification of the heart's affection, so that the bad blood that caused the blemishes is removed.

F. E Marsh

CROSS OF CHRIST: GOLDEN AND BLACK

God is light (1 John 1:5).

God is love (1 John 4:8).

God is light and God is love shine out from the cross of Christ with unmistakable meaning and luster. There sin's desert and sin's Deliverer are seen. One has said of that cross in using the sign of the cross on the dome of London's cathedral:

"There are voices which say that our civilization is a failure. If it has been a failure, the reason is that men have not allowed our social system to feel sufficiently the effect of the Cross. I have sometimes thought, as I saw the great dome of St. Paul's, like a mighty hand holding its gilded cross over the city, that this cross is a cruel and bitter sarcasm. Down below, competition goes on as fiercely as if Christ had never lived or died. Does not that cross sometimes wear a threatening look? When Savonarola was in the midst of his work for Florence he saw, in a dream, a black cross, and upon it were the words, *'Crux iræ Dei'* ('the cross of the wrath of God'). Round it were thunders, lightnings, rain, and hail. In some moods that cross in the city seems to be there for judgment and for judgment alone. But in another vision we remember that Savonarola saw a golden cross with the words, *'Crux misericordiæ Dei'* ('the cross of the mercy of God'), and bright rays streamed down from it into the darkness. That is the vision we must not allow to fade."

Do we not see that the holiness, righteousness, and love of God mingle at the cross of Christ's death? See how these are manifest in the epistle to the Romans.

1. **Righteousness**. "Whom God hath set forth to be a propitiation [satisfaction] through faith in his blood, to declare his righteousness" (3:25).

2. **Abandonment**. "Who was delivered [up] for our offences" (4:25).

3. **Love**. "God commendeth his love . . . Christ died for us" (5:8).

4. **Judgment**. "God . . . condemned sin in the flesh" (8:3).

5. **Grace**. "He that spared not his own Son . . . with him also freely give us all things" (8:32).

F. E. Marsh

CHRIST'S SEVENFOLD CHARACTER

Luke 1:5–17, 26–33, 35; 2:25–26, 36–38

1. "The Lord" (1:17).

John's mission was to "make ready a people prepared for the Lord," or, as the Revised Version states, "To make ready for the Lord a people prepared." A Lord for the people to meet their need, and the people for the Lord to be His joy.

2. "Jesus" (1:31; 2:21).

A common name among the Jews, and yet how uncommon because of Him who bears it.

3. "Son of the Most High" (1:32 RV).

The first time God is called "the Most High God" is in Genesis 14:18–20, and as such He is the "possessor of heaven and earth." Coupled with the statement of the angel regarding Christ as "the Son of the Most High," we see how He illustrates the original title, for as such He will be "great," have the throne of His father David, reign over the house of Jacob, and have an unending kingdom. Ponder the seven "shalts" and "shalls" of verses 31–33.

4. "The Son of God" (1:35).

Christ was God the Son before He became the Son of God; that is, in the essence of His being He was eternally the Son of God, but when the Father would express Himself in human form He became a Son.

5. "The Consolation of Israel" (2:25).

"Consolation" means something or someone near who encourages, enables, and helps us along, hence to console or comfort. The words "comfort" and "consolation" occur a total of ten times in 2 Corinthians 1:3–7.

6. "The Lord's Christ" (2:26).

When the aged Simeon took up the infant Christ in his arms he saw not only "the Lord's Christ" in the infant, but also the "salvation" (v. 30), and the "light to lighten the Gentiles, and the glory of . . . Israel" (v. 32).

7. "Redemption" (2:38).

Christ has paid the price by His precious blood that He might set us at liberty (Eph. 1:7). He frees us from sin's penalty and power, and will ultimately free us from sin's presence.

F. E. Marsh

CHRIST'S RESURRECTION PROCLAIMED

No one can read through the book of the Acts without being convinced that Christ's resurrection is the predominating theme of its witness.

1. Luke opens his treatise by **affirming** it (1:3).

2. Matthias is added to the apostleship that he may **bear witness** to it (1:23).

3. Peter, on the Day of Pentecost, unfolds certain Old Testament Scriptures as **embodying the fact** (3:21–22), and affirms the same fact in connection with the healing of the lame man (3:15).

4. The first persecution was caused by the **declaration** of Christ's resurrection (4:2, 10, 33).

5. Peter **preached** the resurrection of Christ again and again (5:29–32; 10:39–41).

6. Paul is constant in his **testimony** to the resurrection of Christ (Acts 13:30–38; 17:31; 23:6–10; 24:15, 21; 26:23).

F. E. Marsh

CHRIST'S WORDS

Our Lord emphasizes the importance and influence of "words." His words are:

1. **God-given** in their origin (John 17:8).

2. **Life-giving** in their nature (John 6:63, 69).

3. **Faith-producing** in their influence (John 8:30).

4. **Prayer-inspiring** in their working (John 15:7).

5. **Peace-assuring** in their benediction (Luke 24:36–44).

6. **Soul-sustaining** in their intercession (John 18:1).

7. **Wonder-begetting** in their ministry (Luke 4:22; 24:8).

F. E. Marsh

THE ASCENSION OF CHRIST
(ASCENSION DAY)

While they beheld, he was taken up; and a cloud received him out of their sight (Acts 1:9).

His ascension was the last link of that golden chain of events connected with the life and works of Christ here upon earth.

I. The Time of the Ascension.

Forty days after the Resurrection. He remained long enough that His disciples might be certain of His identity and resurrection. Also that He might instruct and qualify them for their great future work and undertakings.

II. The Place of the Ascension.

It was from the Mount of Olives, near Jerusalem. Many important events of the life of Christ are connected with that mountain and vicinity.

III. The Manner of His Ascension.

He led His disciples out as far as Bethany, lifted up His hands and blessed them. "While they beheld, he was taken up; and a cloud received him out of their sight." The ascension was local, visible, real. The disciples saw Him ascend, and two angels attested to the same fact.

IV. The Place to Which He Ascended, and the Grand Designs of Christ's Ascension.

The angels stated that He ascended into heaven. Among the designs were such as these:

A. To show that He had finished His mediatorial work on earth.

B. To represent His people in heaven on their behalf.

C. That He might send down His Holy Spirit, which He did.

D. That He might exercise dominion and receive the homage of both worlds (Eph. 1:21–22; Rev. 5:9).

E. Also He ascended that He might receive to Himself, as Lord of life and death, the spirits of His departed saints. He alone opens the gates of paradise and crowns His people with life eternal.

Let us rejoice in His ascension and gladly place ourselves and all our interests in His hands.

Selected

LIFE BEYOND

Things to come (1 Cor. 3:22).

It has often been said that Christ did not say much about life after death. A well-known preacher has said:

"Christ said little about personal revival or reunion after death, but much about the life that is lived with God and in God, the life that is our spiritual goal, and in the full possession of which is all the good that mind can conceive or heart desire."

Did not Christ say a great deal about "survival" after this life, and the condition of those who have passed on?

Let the following seven Scriptures speak for themselves:

1. Christ's Warning.

"Fear not them which kill the body, but are not able to kill the soul" (Matt. 10:28). Here the soul stands for the individual, which He says man cannot kill.

2. Christ's Statement regarding the unchanging condition of those who "die in [their] sins," who "cannot" come where He is (John 8:21).

He also says they may "seek" Him, but He will not be found. They are in existence or they could not seek Him.

3. Christ on an Eternal Issue.

He speaks of those who believe in Him, and those who will not. "He that believeth on the Son hath everlasting life: and he that believeth not the Son shall not see life; but the wrath of God abideth on him" (John 3:36). The unbeliever may "see" many things, as Dives did (Luke 16:23), but he will not see life. And, further, the eternal present of the "abideth" shows the unbeliever is in existence, and that eternally.

4. Christ's Declaration.

The reason why God, in His love, gave Him was that we should not perish" (John 3:16). Not to receive the Son in His redemptive atonement and remedial grace is to be marred forever, for that is the meaning of "perish" and not annihilation.

5. Christ's Word.

He is uncompromising as to the possibility of committing an "eternal sin," the sin of blasphemy against the Holy Spirit (Matt.

12:31–32 RV). That statement is meaningless if the person is not eternally present.

6. Christ's Promise to His Own.

In speaking of the purpose of His return for them, He said, "I will come again, and receive you unto myself" (John 14:3). This stirring promise is the cheering hope amid the darkness and trials of life, and gilds them with the gold of recompense.

7. Christ's Last Prayer.

In praying for His disciples, He pleaded for His own. He also willed to them His glory, for His word is, "Father, I will that they . . . whom thou hast given me, be with me where I am; that they may behold my glory" (John 17:24). In these words, He did more than express a wish; He set forth His last will and testament.

All the above plainly prove a life beyond the present one, both for the believer and the unbeliever.

F. E. Marsh

THE HOPE OF THE SECOND COMING

1. A **good** hope (2 Thess. 2:16).

2. A **blessed** hope (Titus 2:13).

3. A **joyful** hope (Rom. 5:3; Heb. 3:6).

4. A **sure, firm** hope (Heb. 6:18).

5. A **living** or **lively** hope (1 Peter 1:3).

6. A **saving** hope (Rom. 8:24).

7. A **glorious** hope (Col. 1:27).

8. A **purifying** hope (1 John 3:3).

Selected

COMING WITH CLOUDS

Behold, he cometh with clouds; and every eye shall see him, and they also which pierced him: and all kindreds of the earth shall wail because of him. Even so, Amen (Rev. 1:7).

I. Our Lord Jesus Comes.

A. This fact is worthy of a note of admiration—"Behold!"

B. It should be vividly realized until we cry, "Behold, he cometh!"

C. It should be zealously proclaimed. We should use the herald's cry, "Behold!"

D. It is to be unquestioningly asserted as true. Assuredly He is coming!

    1. It has been long foretold—Enoch (Jude 14).

    2. He has Himself warned us of it—"Behold, I come quickly" (Rev. 3:11).

    3. He has made the sacred supper a token of it—"till he come" (1 Cor. 11:26).

E. It is to be viewed with immediate interest.

    1. "Behold!" for this is the grandest of all events.

    2. "He cometh," the event is at the door.

    3. "He" who is your Lord and Bridegroom comes.

F. It is to be attended with a peculiar sign—"with clouds."

    1. The clouds are the distinctive tokens of His Second Advent.

    2. The tokens of the divine presence—"the dust of His feet" (Nah. 1:3).

    3. The pillar of cloud was such in the wilderness.

    4. The emblems of His majesty.

    5. The ensigns of His power.

    6. The warnings of His judgment. These gathered clouds are charged with darkness and tempest.

II. Our Lord's Coming Will Be Seen by All.

A. It will be a literal appearance. Not merely every mind shall think of Him, but "every eye shall see Him."

B. It will be beheld by all sorts and kinds of living men.

C. It will be seen by those long dead.

D. It will be seen by His actual murderers, and others like them.

E. It will be manifest to those who desire not to see the Lord.

F. It will be a sight in which you will have a share.

III. His Coming Will Cause Sorrow.

"All kindreds of the earth shall wail because of him."

A. The sorrow will be very general—"all kindreds of the earth."

B. The sorrow will be very bitter—"wail."

C. The sorrow proves that men will not be universally converted.

D. The sorrow also shows that men will not expect from Christ's coming a great deliverance.

    1. They will not look to escape from punishment.

    2. They will not look for annihilation.

    3. They will not look for restoration.

    4. If they did so, His coming would not cause them to wail.

E. The sorrow will, in a measure, arise out of His glory, seeing they rejected and resisted Him. That glory will be against them.

> Even so, Lord Jesus, come quickly! In the meanwhile, it is not heaven that can keep You from me; it is not earth that can keep me from You. Raise up my soul to a life of faith with You. Let me even enjoy Your conversation while I expect Your return.
>
> —*Bishop Hall*

"Every eye shall see Him." Every eye—the eye of every living man, whoever he is. None will be able to prevent it. The voice of the trumpet, the brightness of the flame, shall direct all eyes to *Him,* shall fix all eyes upon Him. Be it ever so busy an eye or ever so vain an eye, whatever employment, whatever amusement it had the moment before, will then no longer be able to employ it or to amuse it. The eye will be lifted up to Christ and will no more look down upon money, upon books, upon land, upon houses, upon gardens.

> Your eyes and mine. O awful thought! Blessed Jesus! May we not see You as through tears; may we not then tremble at the sight!
>
> —*Dr. Doddridge*

"And the Lord turned, and looked upon Peter. . . . And Peter went out, and wept bitterly" (Luke 22:61–62). So shall it be, but in a different sense, with sinners at the day of judgment. The eye of Jesus as their Judge shall be fixed upon them, and the look shall awake their sleeping memories and reveal their burdens of sin and shame—countless and cursed crimes, denials worse than Peter's, since lifelong and unrepented of, scoffings at love that wooed them, and despisings of mercy that called them—all these shall pierce their hearts as they behold the look of Jesus.

Spurgeon

Christ's Coming as Viewed by Paul

13. But I would not have you to be ignorant, brethren, concerning them which are asleep, that ye sorrow not, even as others which have no hope.

14. For if we believe that Jesus died and rose again, even so them also which sleep in Jesus will God bring with him.

15. For this we say unto you by the word of the Lord, that we which are alive and remain unto the coming of the Lord, shall not prevent them which are asleep.

16. For the Lord himself shall descend from heaven with a shout, with the voice of the archangel, and with the trump of God: and the dead in Christ shall rise first:

17. Then we which are alive and remain shall be caught up together with them in the clouds, to meet the Lord in the air: and so shall we ever be with the Lord.

18. Wherefore comfort one another with these words.

5 But of the times and the seasons, brethren, ye have no need that I write unto you.

2. For yourselves know perfectly that the day of the Lord so cometh as a thief in the night.

3. For when they shall say, Peace and safety; then sudden destruction cometh upon them, as travail upon a woman with child; and they shall not escape.

4. But ye, brethren, are not in darkness, that that day should overtake you as a thief.

5. We are all the children of light, and the children of the day: we are not of the night, nor of darkness.

6. Therefore let us not sleep, as do others; but let us watch and be sober.

7. For they that sleep sleep in the night; and they that be drunken are drunken in the night.

8. But let us, who are of the day, be sober, putting on the breastplate of faith and love; and for an helmet, the hope of salvation.

9. For God hath not appointed us to wrath, but to obtain salvation by our Lord Jesus Christ,

10. Who died for us, that, whether we wake or sleep, we should live together with him.

11. Wherefore comfort yourselves together, and edify one another, even as also ye do.

12. And we beseech you, brethren, to know them which labour among you, and are over you in the Lord, and admonish you;

13. And to esteem them very highly in love for their work's sake. And be at peace among yourselves.

1 Thessalonians 4:13–5:13

THE MARRIAGE SUPPER OF THE LAMB

And he saith unto me, Write, Blessed are they which are called unto the marriage supper of the Lamb (Rev. 19:9).

I. The Description of the Bridegroom.
The inspired apostle speaks of Him as "the Lamb."

This is John's special name for his Lord. Perhaps he learned it from hearing the Baptist cry by the Jordan, "Behold the Lamb."

A. As the Lamb He is the one everlasting sacrifice for sin; He will not be other than this in His glory.

B. As the Lamb, suffering for sin, He is specially glorious in the eyes of the angels and all other holy intelligence, and so in His joyous day He wears that character.

C. As the Lamb He most fully displays His love to His church, and so He appears in this form on the day of His love's triumph.

D. As the Lamb He is the best loved of our souls. Behold, how He loved us even to the death!

II. The Meaning of the Marriage Supper.
A. The completion and perfection of the church—"His bride has made herself ready" (Rev. 19:7 NIV).

B. The rising of the church into the nearest and happiest communion with Christ in His glory.

C. The commencement of an eternally unbroken rest—"He will rest in His love" (Zeph. 3:17). The church, like Ruth, shall find rest in the house of her husband.

III. The Persons Who Are Called to It.
A. Those who are so called as to accept the invitation.

B. Those who now possess the faith that is the token of admission.

C. Those who love the Bridegroom and bride.

D. Those who have on the wedding garment of sanctification.

E. Those who watch with lamps burning.

IV. The Blessedness That Is Ascribed to Them.
A. They will be blessed indeed when at that feast, for:
1. Those who are called will be admitted.
2. Those who are admitted will be married.

3. Those who are married to Jesus will be endlessly happy. How many a marriage leads to misery? But it is not so in this case!

    B. Alas, some are not thus blessed. To be unblessed is to be accursed.

> He who once hung so sad upon the cross for everyone will look around that bright company, and in every white robe and in every lighted countenance, He will behold the fruit of His sufferings. He will "see of the travail of His soul, and shall be satisfied" (Isa. 53:11). It will be the eternal union of God fulfilled in its deepest counsel—a people given to Christ from before all worlds. They are, that day, all chosen—all gathered—all washed—all saved—and not one of them is lost?
>
> *—James Vaughan*

We dare not say that our Lord will love us more than He loves us now, but He will indulge His love for us more. He will manifest it more, and we shall see more of it and shall understand it better. It will appear to us as though He loved us more. He will lay open His whole heart and soul to us with all its feelings and secrets and purposes, and He will allow us to know them, at least as far as we can understand them. It will contribute to our happiness to know them. The love of this hour will be the perfection of love. This marriage feast will be the feast, the triumph, of love—the exalted Savior showing to the whole universe that He loves us to the utmost boundary love can go, and we loving Him with a fervor, a gratitude, an adoration, and a delight that are new even in heaven.

Spurgeon

O Sacred Head Now Wounded

O sacred Head, now wounded, with grief and shame weighed down, now scornfully surrounded with thorns Thy only crown; how art Thou pale with anguish, with sore abuse and scorn! How does that visage languish which once was bright as morn!

What Thou, my Lord, hast suffered was all for sinners' gain. Mine, mine was the transgression, but Thine the deadly pain. Lo, here I fall, my Savior! 'Tis I deserve Thy place; look on me with Thy favor; vouch-safe to me Thy grace.

What language shall I borrow to thank Thee, dearest Friend, for this Thy dying sorrow, Thy pity without end? O make me Thine forever! And, should I fainting be, Lord, let me never, never outlive my love to Thee!

Bernard of Clairvaux

It doth not yet appear what we shall be: but we know that, when he shall appear, we shall be like him; for we shall see him as he is (1 John 3:2).

I. **"It Doth Not Yet Appear What We Shall Be."**
   At present we are veiled and travel through the world *incognito.*
   A. Our Master was not made manifest here below.
      1. His glory was veiled in flesh.
      2. His Deity was concealed in infirmity.
      3. His power was hidden under sorrow and weakness.
      4. His riches were buried under poverty and shame.
      5. The world knew Him not, for He was made flesh.

   B. We must have an evening before our morning, undergraduate work before our college, a tuning before the music is ready.

   C. This is not the time in which to appear in our glory.
      1. The winter prepares flowers, but does not call them forth.
      2. The ebb-tide reveals the secrets of the sea, but many of our rivers no gallant ship can then sail.
      3. To everything there is a season, and this is not the time of glory.

II. **"But We Know That, When He Shall Appear."**
   A. We speak of our Lord's manifestation without doubt—"we know."

   B. Our faith is so assured that it becomes knowledge.

   C. He will be manifest upon this earth in person.

III. **"We Shall Be Like Him."**
   A. Having a body like His body.
   Sinless, incorruptible, painless, spiritual, clothed with beauty and power, and yet most real and true.

   B. Having a soul like His soul.
   Perfect, holy, instructed, developed, strengthened, active, delivered from temptation, conflict, and suffering.

   C. Having such dignities and glories as He wears.
   Kings, priests, conquerors, judges, sons of God.

IV. **"We Shall See Him As He Is."**
   A. This glorious sight will perfect our likeness.
   B. This will be the result of our being like Him.

C. This will be evidence of our being like Him, since none but the pure in heart can see God.
1. The sight will be ravishing.
2. The sight will be transforming and transfiguring.
3. The sight will be abiding and a source of bliss forever.

> God showed *power* in making us creatures, but *love* in making us sons. Plato gave God thanks that He had made him a man and not a beast; but what cause have they to adore God's love who has made them children! The apostle puts an Amen! to it, *Behold!*
>
> —*Thomas Watson*

Such divine, God-given glimpses into the future reveal to us more than all our thinking. What intense truth, what divine meaning there is in God's creative word: "Let us make man in our image, after our likeness"! (Gen. 1:26). To show forth the likeness of the invisible, to be partaker of the divine nature, to share with God His rule of the universe is man's destiny. His place is indeed one of unspeakable glory.

> Standing between two eternities, the eternal purpose in which we were predestined to be conformed to the image of the first-born Son, and the eternal realization of that purpose, when we shall be like Him in His glory. We hear the voice from every side: O image bearers of God! on the way to share the glory of God and of Christ, live a Godlike, live a Christlike life!
>
> —*Andrew Murray*

A converted blind man once said, "Jesus Christ will be the first person I shall ever see, for my eyes will be opened in heaven."

"You are going to be with Jesus, and to see Him as He is," said a friend to Rowland Hill on his deathbed. "Yes," replied Mr. Hill, with emphasis, "and I shall be *like* Him; *that* is the crowning point."

Spurgeon

THE MANNER OF THE SECOND COMING

Revelation 22:20

Christ is coming:

1. In the Clouds.
"And they shall see the Son of man coming in the clouds of heaven" (Matt. 24:30; see 26:64; Rev. 1:7).

2. In the Glory of His Father.
"For the Son of man shall come in the glory of his Father" (Matt. 16:27).

3. In His Own Glory.
"When the Son of man shall come in his glory" (Matt. 25:31).

4. In Flaming Fire.
"And to you who are troubled rest with us, when the Lord Jesus shall be revealed from heaven with his mighty angels, in flaming fire taking vengeance on them that know not God, and that obey not the gospel of our Lord Jesus Christ" (2 Thess. 1:7–8).

5. With Great Power.
"And they shall see the Son of man coming in the clouds of heaven with power and great glory" (Matt. 24:30; see 28:18).

6. With His Angels.
"For the Son of man shall come in the glory of his Father with his angels" (Matt. 16:27; see 25:31; Mark 8:38; 2 Thess. 1:7).

7. With a Shout.
"For the Lord himself shall descend from heaven with a shout, with the voice of the archangel, and with the trump of God" (1 Thess. 4:16).

8. With His Saints.
"And the Lord make you to increase and abound in love one toward another, and toward all men, even as we do toward you: to the end he may stablish your hearts unblameable in holiness before God, even our Father, at the coming of our Lord Jesus Christ with all his saints" (1 Thess. 3:12–13).

9. As a Thief.
"Behold, I come as a thief. Blessed is he that watcheth, and

keepeth his garments, lest he walk naked, and they see his shame" (Rev. 16:15; see 1 Thess 5:2; 2 Peter 3:10).

10. As the Lightning.

"For as the lightning cometh out of the east, and shineth even unto the west; so shall also the coming of the Son of man be" (Matt. 24:27).

11. As He Ascended.

"And when he had spoken these things, while they beheld, he was taken up; and a cloud received him out of their sight. And while they looked stedfastly toward heaven as he went up, behold, two men stood by them in white apparel; which also said, Ye men of Galilee, why stand ye gazing up into heaven? this same Jesus, which is taken up from you into heaven, shall so come in like manner as ye have seen him go into heaven" (Acts 1:9–11).

12. Suddenly.

"Lest coming suddenly he find you (Mark 13:36; see Rev. 22:20).

13. Unexpectedly.

"Therefore be ye also ready: for in such an hour as ye think not the Son of man cometh" (Matt. 24:44; see v. 42; Luke 12:40).

"Watch therefore, for ye know neither the day nor the hour wherein the Son of man cometh" (Matt. 25:13).

Wm. Schweinfurth

The Manner of His Coming

12. And behold, I come quickly; and my reward is with me, to give every man according as his work shall be.

13. I am Alpha and Omega, the beginning and the end, the first and the last.

14. Blessed are they that do his commandments, that they may have right to the tree of life, and may enter in through the gates into the city.

15. For without are dogs, and sorcerers, and whoremongers, and murderers, and idolaters, and whosoever loveth and maketh a lie.

16. I Jesus have sent mine angel to testify unto you these things in the churches. I am the root and the offspring of David, and the bright and morning Star.

17. And the Spirit and the bride say, Come.

And let him that heareth say, Come. And let him that is athirst come. And whosoever will, let him take the water of life freely.

18. For I testify unto every man that heareth the words of the prophecy of this book, If any man shall add unto these things, God shall add unto him the plagues that are written in this book:

19. And if any man shall take away from the words of the book of this prophecy, God shall take away his part out of the book of life, and out of the holy city, and from the things which are written in this book.

20. He which testifieth these things saith, Surely I come quickly. Amen. Even so, come, Lord Jesus.

Revelation 22:12–20

CHRIST'S CONQUESTS IN THE
BOOK OF THE REVELATION

The one predominating thought in the book of the Revelation is the Lamb, in all the livingness of His death, puts down His foes and reigns over His enemies. The wounded One of Calvary is the Warrior conquering His enemies. The book of the unveiling is the revelation that:

1. God's Little Lamb shall conquer **the red dragon** of hell (12:9–13).

2. He will put down the **seven-headed and ten-horned beast** of a revived Roman Empire (17:12–14).

3. He will blast **the false prophet of Antichrist** by the brightness of His coming (19:20).

4. He will cause the **corrupt woman** of Christendom to be slaughtered by the confederates (17:15–18).

5. He will wipe out the sin-riddled and **demon-possessed city** of Babylon (18:16-24).

6. He will break **the nations** who oppose Him with the rod of His power (19:11–15).

7. He will **remove all who stand in the way** of His sway as He merges the kingdoms of the world to crown Him King of Kings and Lord of Lords.

The Lamb that was slain is the Conqueror. He was once trodden in the winepress because of man's sin, and because of this He shall conquer His enemies as He treads them down in the fierceness of God's wrath (19:16–18).

F. E. Marsh

CHRIST'S COMING INTRODUCES
THE MILLENNIUM

There are many portions of Scripture that foretell what will take place when Christ returns, but we concentrate upon what the Lord will do in connection with two phrases that occur several times in the prophecy of Isaiah, namely, "the Lord shall come" or "will come." The expression is connected with two thoughts: overthrow of His enemies and the inauguration of the Millennium. As the Lord of Hosts, He will come to fight for Mount Zion and to defend His people. He will not only defend Jerusalem, but He will pass all over it, as a mother bird hides her young under her wings to protect them (Isa. 31:4–5).

1. As the **Bringer of Blessings**, He says He will come and save, and there are many blessings that shall ensue as a result of His coming. See the twenty "shalls" in Isaiah 35:4–10 (RV).

2. As the **Mighty One**, He will come to rule His flock like a shepherd (Isa. 40:10–11). The eastern sheik was the one that not only tended his flock, but ruled his own household. When our Lord comes His arm shall rule, and He shall feed His flock like a shepherd.

3. As the **Redeemer**, He will come to Zion to turn away ungodliness from Jacob (Isa. 59:20). Birks renders "come to Zion," "for the sake of Zion," or "out of Zion," as in Romans 11:26. The Hebrew is "for" in the sense "on behalf of." The thought undoubtedly is, He comes to give deliverance from transgression and ungodliness.

4. As the **Avenger**, the Lord will come with fire to overthrow the enemies of His people and to plead with all flesh; and following this, He brings in the new heavens and the new earth, and He shall cause the children of Israel to be brought by the nations as an offering to the Lord, and all flesh shall worship Him (Isa. 66:15–23).

F. E. Marsh

THE LORD'S COMING

Its practical bearing:

1. **Upon Creation** (Isa. 35:1; 55:13; Rom. 8:19–23).

2. **Upon the Gentiles or Nations** (Isa. 11:4; Jer. 3:17; Zech. 14:16; Acts 15:16–17).

3. **Upon Israel** (Isa. 8:23; 12:10; Jer. 16:14–15; Rom. 11:1, 26).

4. **Upon the Believer**. Salvation is not complete until He comes (Rom. 8:23; Phil. 3:20–21; 1 Peter 1:3–5).
    a. It is the blessed hope (Titus 2:13).
    b. A course of comfort (1 Thess. 4:13–18).
    c. Purifies (Col. 3:1–5; 1 John 3:2–3).
    d. Should make the believer patient (Heb. 10:36–37; James 5:7–8).
    e. Charitable (1 Cor. 4:5).
    f. Sincere (Phil. 1:9–10).
    g. Faithful (Luke 12:43; 2 Tim. 4:1–2).
    h. Yielding and moderate (Phil 4:5).
    i. Watchful and sober (1 Peter 4:7).
    j. Abiding (1 John 2:28).
    k. Sustains in tribulation (2 Peter 1:7; 4:13).
    l. An incentive to holiness and separation (Titus 2:11–13; 2 Peter 3:10–12).

Luther Rees

THREEFOLD WORK OF CHRIST

1. **Atonement:** Past—on the cross.

2. **Advocacy:** Present—before the throne.

3. **Advent:** Future—at His coming.

A. M. Clemence

THREE OFFICES OF THE LORD JESUS

1. **Savior** (Luke 2:11)—Past.

2. **Priest** (Heb. 4:14)—Present.

3. **Bridegroom** (Matt. 25:6)—Future.

OCCUPY

We read in Luke 19:13 Jesus' challenge to His servants: "Occupy till I come."

1. Occupy—the Responsibility is **Immense** (1 Peter 4:10).

2. Till—the Return is **Indefinite** (Matt. 24:36).

3. I—the Redeemer is **Infinite** (John 8:59).

4. Come—the Return Is **Imminent** (John 14:3).

READY WHEN HE COMES

Matthew 24:33, 44, 46

1. Doing His will—obedient (John 14:23).

2. Not defiling our separation (2 Cor. 6:14).

3. Not forsaking pilgrim character (John 17:13).

4. Going forth without the camp (Heb. 13:13).

5. Witnessing for Christ (Acts 1:8).

6. Affections on things above (Col. 3:1).

7. Laying up treasure in heaven (Matt. 6:19).

Franklin Ferguson

FOUR GLORIOUS FACTS ABOUT OUR LORD

1. **He Died**—"Dead already" (Mark 15:44).

2. **He Rose**—"Risen indeed" (Luke 24:34).

3. **He Lives**—"Alive evermore" (Rev. 1:18).

4. **He Comes**—"Coming quickly" (Rev. 22:20).

Hy Pickering

HE SHALL BE GREAT

Luke 1:32

1. Great in His preexistent glory.

2. Great as Creator coequal with God the Father.

3. All great prophesies relate to this great One.

4. All great types relate to Him.

5. His great coming to put away sin the greatest event up to date in world's history.

6. Greatest life character and example of all ages.

7. Great Savior, great sacrifice, great salvation.

8. Great in resurrection power.

9. Great in glory as mediator, advocate, and intercessor.

10. Great coming King and kingdom.

James Spink

CHRIST'S RETURN

A Presbyterian minister said to the writer, "I was never taught anything about the return of the Lord when I was in the theological college." Then he asked me about the best book on the theme, and I immediately replied, "The New Testament." No one can read through that book without being convinced of the following:

1. That Christ is personally coming back again, **as He promised** (John 14:1–3).

2. That His coming is **premillennial,** that is, before the kingdom of righteousness can be ushered in, the King must return (Luke 19:12).

3. That He has committed to His servants the pound of the Gospel, with which they are **to trade** until His return (Luke 19:13–14).

4. That the Lord's purpose in this dispensation is not to convert the world, but **to gather out** a people for His Name (Acts 15:13–18).

5. That **evil will abound** and increase under the rule of man and the god of this world (2 Tim. 3:1–9).

6. That Christ will come for His people and **remove them** from the world, and raise the blessed dead before He comes with them in judgment (1 Thess. 4:13–18).

7. That Christ will **destroy the Man of Sin** by His personal appearing and overthrow all the forces of evil (2 Thess. 2:8).

F. E. Marsh

CHRIST'S COMING AND OUR RESPONSIBILITY

Luke 12:35–48

1. **Announcement** of His coming—"when he cometh" (v. 36).

2. **Watching** for His coming—"shall find watching" (v. 37).

3. **Reward** of His coming—"will come forth and serve them" (v. 37).

4. **Blessedness** of His coming—"blessed are those servants" (v. 38).

5. **Loss,** if not ready for His coming (v. 39).

6. **Command** about His coming—"be ye therefore ready" (v. 40).

7. **Faithfulness** and reward *re* His coming (vv. 42–44).

8. **Effect** of not expecting His coming (v. 45).

9. **Judgment** upon those who are not ready for His coming (vv. 46–48).

F. E. Marsh

For Me

Amid a rabble cry,
Under an Eastern sky,
A Man went forth to die
  For me!

Thorn-crowned His blessed head,
Blood-stained His every tread,
Cross-laden on He sped,
  For me!

Pierced through His hands and feet,
Three hours o'er Him did beat
Fierce rays of noontide heat,
  For me!

Thus wert Thou made all mine,
Lord, make me wholly Thine,
Give grace and strength divine
  To me!

In thought and word and deed,
Thy will to do; oh! lead my feet
E'en though they bleed
  To Thee.

Author Unknown

"PREPARE YE THE WAY OF THE LORD"

Matthew 3:1–10

Introduction

These words addressed to individuals, institutions, and nations.

    A. Pharisees.

    B. Sadducees.

    C. All the multitude.

I. A Dispensational Preparation.

There are seasons of special divine manifestation. God has a plan and mode of manifestations; not uniform and staid, but always timely and proper. Prepare to cooperate with God's plan.

II. A Personal Preparation.

    A. Repentance.

    B. Correction of conduct.

    C. Self-effacement—full surrender. No confidence in race, ancestry, or position.

    D. This personal preparation is prerequisite to His coming, not the result of His coming.

III. God's Eternal Principles of Preparation Are Immutable.

IV. God Is Coming—Whether We Are Prepared for Him or Not.

"Who may abide the day of his coming?" (Mal. 3:2).

Fred Reedy

WATCHMAN, WHAT OF THE NIGHT?

Isaiah 21:11

1. The night is far spent (Rom. 13:12).

2. The Lord is at hand (James 5:8 RV).

3. He comes quickly (Rev. 22:12, 20).

4. Therefore let us not sleep (1 Thess. 5:6).

5. But watch and be sober (1 Peter 4:7).

6. Looking for the glorious appearing of our Lord Jesus Christ (Titus 2:13).

7. When we shall be caught up to meet Him in the air (1 Thess. 4:17).

8. To reign with Him forever (2 Tim. 2:12; Rev. 3:21).
   "Behold I come . . . blessed is he that watcheth, and keepeth his garments" (Rev. 16:15).

Selected

An Hour with Thee

Lord, what a change within us one short hour
   Spent in Thy presence will avail to make!
   What heavy burdens from our bosoms take!
What parched grounds refresh as with a shower!
We kneel, and all around us seems to lower;
   We rise, and all, the distant and the near,
   Stands forth in sunny outline, brave and clear;
We kneel, how weak; we rise, how full of power!
   Why, therefore, should we do ourselves this wrong,
   Or others—that we are not always strong—
That we are sometimes overborne with care—
   That we should ever weak or heartless be,
Anxious or troubled—when with us is prayer,
   And joy and strength and courage are with Thee?

Richard Chenevix Trench

POWER OF CHRIST'S RETURN

In speaking of the sustaining power of a personal faith in the personal return of Christ, Archibald G. Brown said, "If the eyes of faith had not brought me to see the Second Coming of Christ as the fulfillment of prophecy, force of circumstances would have driven me into infidelity. When I see iniquity more and more abounding, more heathen than fifty years ago, less godly and converted people, only this hope sustains me, that He will come again—not the weary one, the despised one—but in power and in might, at His Father's right hand. And woe to the despots then! Then shall begin the Millennial age when He shall appear, showing the wounds of the Lamb that was slain, and when righteousness shall cover the earth. The same Christ, He and not another, and we shall know Him by the print of the nails!" Yes, the "Blessed Hope" of Christ's return is:

1. Our **Comfort** in Sorrow (1 Thess. 4:14).
2. Our **Joy** in Persecution (2 Thess. 1:7).
3. Our **Purifier** in Life (1 John 3:3).
4. Our **Outlook** of Expectation (Phil. 3:20–21).
5. Our **Confidence** in Confession (Heb. 10:23 RV).
6. Our **Patience** in Trial (James 5:7).
7. Our **Strength** in Endurance (1 Peter 1:13).

F. E. Marsh

THE FUTURE OF THE BELIEVER

1. We shall be . . . **changed** (1 Cor. 15:51–52).
2. We shall be . . . **glorified** (Rom. 8:17).
3. We shall be . . . **like Him** (1 John 3:2).
4. We shall be . . . **with Him** (2 Tim. 2:12).
5. We shall . . . **see Him** as He is (1 John 3:2).
6. **Face to face** (1 Cor. 13:12).
7. **In His Beauty** (Isa. 33:17).
8. **Altogether lovely** (Song 5:16).

Selected

WHEN YOU SEE JESUS

Luke 19:1–4

When you see Jesus the results will be:

1. You will see yourself (Isa. 6:5).
It makes a difference by what standard you measure (Acts 9:6; Rev. 3:17).

2. You will turn away from sin (Luke 19:8).
True repentance always flees the old life (Acts 2:38–39; 3:19).

3. You will have a spirit of humility (Luke 22:27).
Most unusual for the natural man (Mark 10:45; Luke 6:27–28, 35).

4. You will seek a higher standard (1 Peter 1:15–16).
You will not be content with the old order (Prov. 4:18; Gal. 2:20).

5. You will be journeying by a new way (Matt. 2:12).
Many a journey has been changed since Christ came (Ps. 40:1–4; Acts 9:20–21).

6. You will be able to see others (Isa. 6:5–9).
Many who never saw the Lord—do not see others (Mark 6:34; Acts 8:4).

7. You will be looking for His return (1 Thess. 1:9–10).
If you have seen Him in Spirit, you will want to meet Him in Person (Heb. 9:28; 1 John 3:1–3).

C. C. Maple

"TILL HE COME"

1. Working (Luke 19:13).

2. Following (John 21:22–23).

3. Remembering (1 Cor. 11:23, 26).

4. Holding Fast (Rev. 2:25).

Selected

THE BLESSEDNESS OF CHRIST'S SECOND COMING (BLESSEDNESS FOR THOSE WHO ARE FOUND WATCHING)

Luke 12:35–48

In the parable of the Lord returning from the wedding, Christ enforces and emphasizes the coming of Himself (Luke 12:35–48). The distinctiveness of our Lord's return is declared no less than nine times in connection with the words: "He cometh," "will come," "come," "The Son of Man cometh," and "He shall come." In relation to the last, our Lord declares that when "He shall come" and find His servants waiting and watching, those servants are "blessed." They shall be "blessed" in many ways:

1. They shall be "blessed" **with His approval,** because they will be ready to "open unto him immediately," when "he cometh and knocketh" (v. 36).

2. They shall be "blessed" **with His service,** for, finding them watching, "he . . . will come forth and serve them" (v. 37).

3. They shall be "blessed" **in not suffering loss,** for Christ implies in the parabolical language used, the man who does not watch against "the thief" finds his house "broken through" (vv. 39–40).

4. They shall be "blessed" **for faithful and wise stewardship** in being appointed rulers over the Lord's household and in ministering to others (vv. 42–44).

The fact that those who are found watching shall be "blessed" implies that those who are not so found will suffer loss and disapproval. Yes, more, those servants will be "beaten with many stripes," who knew their Lord's will and did not "prepare" themselves. Also, those who did not know their Lord's will receive few stripes. Yet again, those who professed to be His servants and presumed upon their position will be "cut" off (vv. 45–48).

F. E. Marsh

WHEN CHRIST SHALL RETURN

Acts 3:20–21; 15:16

1. **The dead in Christ shall be raised** (1 Thess. 4:16).
   Known as the first resurrection (not a general resurrection) (Luke 14:14; John 11:23–25; 1 Cor. 15:53; Rev. 20:6).

2. **The living believers shall be changed** (1 Cor. 15:52).
   We will wear the image of the heavenly (1 Cor. 15:49, 53–54; Phil. 3:20–21; 1 John 3:2).

3. **The church (the body of Christ) shall be translated** (1 Thess. 4:17).
   This is the time of the Morning Star (John 14:3; 2 Thess. 2:1; 2 Peter 1:19).

4. **The believer's works are to be judged** (Rom. 14:10).
   This is for the purpose of rewarding (Luke 19:11–26; 1 Cor. 3:10–13; 2 Cor. 5:10).

5. **The Jewish nation shall be restored** (Matt. 24:34).
   The Jews still continue with us and shall (Luke 21:24–33; Acts 15:14–16; Rom. 11:26).

6. **The living nations shall be judged** (Matt. 25:30–31).

7. **The kingdom of God shall be established in all its fullness upon the earth** (Acts 1:6–7).
   Christ shall sit upon David's throne (Isa. 9:7; Dan. 7:13–14, 18, 27; Rev. 3:31).

C. C. Maple

THE LAST PROMISE OF THE LORD JESUS

Acts 1:8–9

1. **A Personal Promise**—"ye," "you."

2. **A Certain Promise**—"ye shall."

3. **A Definite Promise**—"power."

4. **His Last Promise**—"a cloud received him."

Selected

CHRIST'S SECOND COMING

Luke 21:27

Throughout the most solemn and pathetic series of predictions in this chapter, Christ is speaking of two distinct events so simultaneously that it is, at times, difficult to say of which He is speaking. Undoubtedly the destruction of Jerusalem was a true shadow of the great day of judgment, and our Lord's thought appears now to have passed from the nearer judgment upon Jerusalem to a more awful judgment.

It is difficult for us to realize that this judgment will certainly take place. The imagination finds it hard to picture to itself this tremendous collapse—this overwhelming conclusion of all that we see and are most conversant with.

The date of this judgment is in the hands of God. It is one of those times and seasons that He has put in His own power, and it cannot be conjectured by us without risk of folly and disappointment. With God "one day is as a thousand years, and a thousand years as one day." If He seems to delay, it is in His mercy, not in His forgetfulness, still less in His impotence. He is not willing that any should perish.

The last judgment will come home to every one of us as closely as anything possibly can. We shall all see Jesus Christ in His true majesty and glory. We shall all see ourselves as we truly are. The day for disguises and half truths will be past. The ambitions, titles, stations, positions will be nothing to us then.

In presence of the last realties we are all of us alike on an absolute level. Let us learn that all that belongs merely to the things of time, and all that does not lead to God or come from God, is but a surface incident in the history of existence.

H. P. Leiddow

THE SECOND COMING OF CHRIST

Acts 1:11

It means:

1. The Last Time.

"Who are kept by the power of God through faith unto salvation ready to be revealed in the last time" (1 Peter 1:5).

2. The Times of Restitution.

"Whom the heaven must receive until the times of restitution of all things, which God hath spoken by the mouth of all his holy prophets since the world began" (Acts 3:21; see Rom. 8:21).

3. The Times of Refreshing.

"Repent ye therefore, and be converted, that your sins may be blotted out, when the times of refreshing shall come from the presence of the Lord" (Acts 3:19).

4. The Appearing of Jesus Christ.

"That the trial of your faith, being much more precious than of gold that perisheth, though it be tried with fire, might be found unto praise and honour and glory at the appearing of Jesus Christ" (1 Peter 1:7).

5. The Glorious Appearing of the Great God.

"Looking for that blessed hope, and the glorious appearing of the great God and our Saviour Jesus Christ" (Titus 2:13).

6. The Revelation of Jesus Christ.

"Wherefore gird up the loins of your mind, be sober, and hope to the end for the grace that is to be brought unto you at the revelation of Jesus Christ" (1 Peter 1:13).

7. The Day of Our Lord Jesus Christ.

"Who shall also confirm you unto the end, that ye may be blameless in the day of our Lord Jesus Christ" (1 Cor. 1:8; 2 Peter 3:10).

8. The Day of God.

"Looking for and hasting unto the coming of the day of God, wherein the heavens being on fire shall be dissolved, and the elements shall melt with fervent heat?" (2 Peter 3:21).

Wm. Schweinfurth

EVENTS AWAITING THE RETURN OF THE LORD FROM HEAVEN

Acts 3:20–21

1. The resurrection of the dead in Christ (1 Thess. 4:16).
Discuss—first, second, general resurrection (Dan. 12:2; 1 Cor. 15:23; Rev. 20:6).

2. The transfiguration of living believers (1 Cor. 15:52).
Discuss—nature of resurrected body (1 Cor. 15:42; Phil. 3:20–21; 1 John 3:2).

3. The translation of the church (Christ's body) (1 Thess. 4:17).
Discuss—those who see the Morning Star (John 14:3; 2 Thess. 2:1; Heb. 9:28).

4. The judgment of the believer's works (Rom. 10:14).
Discuss—seven New Testament judgments (Luke 19:11–26; 1 Cor. 3:10–15; 2 Cor. 5:10).

5. The restoration of the Jewish nation (Matt. 24:44).
Discuss—the indestructible Jew (Luke 21:24–33; Acts 15:14–18; Rom. 11:18).

6. The judgment of the living nations (Matt. 25:30–31).
Discuss—nations who will enjoy age life (Joel 2:12; Rev. 5:10; 11:18).

7. The establishment of the kingdom of God (2 Tim. 4:1).
Discuss—what the kingdom is *not,* what it *is* (Dan. 7:13; Luke 19:12–13; Rev. 11:21).

> The Kingdom is coming, O tell ye the story,
>   God's banner exalted shall be;
> The earth shall be full of His knowledge and glory,
>   As waters that cover the sea.

C. C. Maple

CHRIST'S RETURN

A minister who was talking with a Christian worker said, "Christ came again twenty years ago, when He came into my heart." Whereupon the Christian worker replied, "I read in my Bible that certain things are to happen when Christ returns and among them, the dead in Christ shall be raised and the living believers in Him will be changed. Have either of these taken place?" The question nonplused the minister! No honest reader of the discourse of Christ as recorded in Matthew 24–25 can deny His word about His coming again.

His return is:

1. **Promised** by Christ (John 14:3).

2. **Declared** by the two men who stood by the disciples when He went away (Acts 1:11).

3. **Announced** by Peter (Acts 3:20).

4. **Described** by Paul (1 Thess. 4:13–18).

5. **Urged** by James (James 5:7).

6. **Affirmed** by John (1 John 3:2).

7. **Quoted** by Jude (v. 14).

F. E. Marsh

THE COMING ONE

John 14:3

1. I—the **Person**.

2. I will—the **Power**.

3. I will come—the **Promise**.

4. I will come again—the **Prospect**.

5. And receive you unto myself—the **People**.

6. That where I am—the **Place**.

7. There ye may be also—the **Purpose**.

Selected

IN MUCH ASSURANCE

John 20:31; 1 Thessalonians 1:3

Key thought: "We know."

1. **Assurance that we belong to Christ** (1 John 2:3, 5).
That we are members of His "flock" (John 10:14; Acts 2:47; 1 John 5:13).

2. **Assurance that He abides in us** (1 John 3:24).
In the words of the song, "Jesus Is Real to Me" (Rom. 8:9; 1 John 4:13).

3. **Assurance that He hears our prayer** (1 John 5:15).
We have access to Him, our Intercessor (Ps. 91:15; John 16:23–24).

4. **Assurance that all things work for good** (Rom. 8:28).
In things for our spiritual good (Ps. 23:1; Phil. 4:19).

5. **Assurance that prophecy is true** (Dan. 2:45).
We can depend upon its guidance to light our way (Matt. 2:5; 2 Peter 1:19).

6. **Assurance of the future life** (Job 19:25).
Christ gave us a demonstration that we may know (John 11:25; Acts 17:31; 1 Cor. 15:22).

7. **Assurance that He shall return** (Heb. 9:28).
That we shall see Him and be like Him (1 Thess. 4:16–17; 1 John 3:2).

C. C. Maple

In a Moment

A moment more and I may be
Caught up in glory, Lord, with Thee:
And, raptured sight, Thy beauty see
For evermore!

A moment more—what joy to wear
Thy likeness, Saviour, and to share
With Thee the place prepared there,
Where Thou art gone!

A moment more—upon Thy throne,
Thy place by right, then made our own;
Thou wilt not fill that seat alone,
But with Thy saints!

Author Unknown

THE SECOND COMING OF CHRIST IN
1 THESSALONIANS

I. The Manner of His Coming.
   A. Personal—"the Lord Himself" (4:16).
   B. Glorious—"clouds," "angels," "trumpets" (4:16).

II. Purpose or Results of His Coming.
   A. To raise sleeping saints from the dead (4:16).
   B. To translate living saints (4:17).
   C. To bring about eternal union with Christ (4:17).
   D. To complete sanctification of believers (3:13; 5:23).
   E. To reward faithful workers (2:19).
   F. To bring sudden destruction on the ungodly (5:3).

III. Time of His Coming.
   A. The exact time cannot and need not be known (5:1–2).
   B. For the wicked, sudden and unexpected (5:3).
   C. Not so necessarily for believers (5:4).
   D. While wickedness still abounds (5:3).

IV. Attitude of Church Toward His Coming.
   A. Ought not to be ignorant of nor slight (1:10; 4:13).
   B. The hope with which to comfort one another in sorrow (4:18).
   C. To be watching for it (5:6).
   D. Should lead to sober, earnest lives (5:4–8).

N. Fay Smith

Rest

Not so in haste, my heart!
Have faith in God and wait:
Although He linger long
He never comes too late.

Until He cometh, rest,
Until He cometh, rest,
Nor grudge the hours that roll,
The feet that wait for God
Are soonest at the goal.

Are soonest at the goal
That is not gained by speed.
Then hold thee still, my heart,
For I shall wait His lead.

Bayard Taylor

HOPE OF THE RESURRECTION

For all who have believed on Christ to the saving of their souls, the hope of the resurrection of the body is:

1. A **comforting** hope (Job 19:25, 27; 1 Thess. 4:13, 18).
2. A **satisfying** hope (Ps. 17:15).
3. A **sustaining** hope (2 Cor. 4:17–18; 5:1, 3).
4. A **lively** hope (1 Peter 1:3, 7).
5. A **glorious** hope (Rom. 8:18).
6. A **sure** hope (John 14:19; Rev. 1:18).
7. A **triumphant** hope (Hos. 13:14; 1 Cor. 15:55).
8. A **jubilant** hope (Isa. 26:19).
9. A **blessed** hope (Rev. 20:6).
10. A **believer's** hope (1 John 2:25).

J. Ellis

THE SECOND COMING OF CHRIST

Hebrews 9:28

Introduction

In God's plan for the salvation of men, Jesus was to come to the earth twice. The first time He came to give His life and shed His blood that we might be saved. The second time He will come in power and glory, "without a sin offering for salvation." We must accept the full benefits of His first coming to be prepared for His second coming, for the joy of His second coming is reserved for those "that look for him," and only those who are prepared are looking for Him in genuine anticipation.

I. Christ's Second Coming Is to Be Personal
(Acts 1:10–11).

His second coming is not to be identified with the coming of the Holy Spirit at Pentecost, with death, with the preaching of the Gospel among the nations or with any other invisible occurrence in the history of men; for His coming is "in like manner" as He went away. That is, it is to be personal and visible to His disciples.

II. The Time of Christ's Second Coming Is at the End of This Age (Matt. 24:14).

From the beginning of the Christian era the second coming of Christ has been imminent, and its approach has greater meaning for us than for any that have lived before us. By imminent we do not mean that Christ will come at some certain time, but rather that He may come at any time. We may not know the exact time of His coming; this knowledge is in the mind of God. But the Scriptures give certain signs that are to indicate that His coming draws near. These signs are:

    A. Lukewarmness in the church (Matt. 24:12; 2 Tim. 3:1–5).

    B. Distress and uncertainty among the nations (Matt. 24:7).

    C. Want of equity in the economic sphere (James 5:1–8).

    D. The general deterioration of the traditional family (2 Tim. 3:2).

III. The Manner and Purpose of His Coming

(1 Thess. 4:13–17).

    A. The Lord shall descend with a shout. The coming will be sudden, personal, and glorious.

    B. The dead in Christ shall be resurrected, and the living in Christ shall be translated.

    C. The saved of the ages, constituting the church, the bride, the Lamb's wife, will go on to the marriage supper of the Lamb (Rev. 19:7–9).

    D. The Great Tribulation shall then come to the earth (Rev. 16–19).

IV. Preparation for His Coming (Matt. 24:44).

To the Master's word, "Surely, I come quickly," does your heart respond, "Amen. Even so, come Lord Jesus"?

J. B. Chapman

WHY CHRIST WILL COME AGAIN

Hebrews 9:28

1. To take His own to be with Him forever (John 14:1–3; 1 Thess. 4:17).

2. To complete our salvation (Rom. 8:21–23; 1 Peter 1:5).

3. To be the Judge of all (Matt. 25:32; Acts 17:31; Rom. 2:16).

4. To be glorified in His saints (Mark 9:2–3; 2 Thess. 1:10).

5. To have us appear with Him in glory (Luke 12:37; Col. 3:4).

6. To establish us in perfect holiness (1 Thess. 3:13).

7. To transform us in His own image (1 Cor. 15:52; Phil. 3:20–21).

Selected

"HE THAT SHALL COME WILL COME, AND WILL NOT TARRY"

Hebrews 10:37

1. "Behold, I come quickly" (Rev. 3:11).

2. "Behold, . . . my reward is with me" (Rev. 22:12).

3. "Blessed is he that watcheth and keepeth his garments" (Rev. 16:15).

4. "Be watchful. . . . If thou shalt not watch, I will come on thee as a thief, and thou shalt not know what hour I will come upon thee" (Rev. 3:2–3).

Selected

THE BLESSED HOPE

Titus 2:13

1. Christ, the Hope of glory (Col. 1:27; Heb. 6:19).

2. We hope for His return (John 14:1–3; Eph. 1:13).

3. He will come to gather His own (1 Cor. 15:52).

4. We will enter in our possession (Eph. 1:18).

5. It is a happy hope (Heb. 3:6; 1 John 3:3).

6. We rejoice in this hope (Rom. 5:2; 12:12).

7. We hope in His holy promises (Acts 26:6–7; Phil. 3:20–21; Titus 1:2).

Selected

FOUR TRUTHS THAT NEED EMPHASIS IN THESE LATTER DAYS

2 Timothy 4:2

1. The inspired Word (John 5:39; 6:63; 2 Tim. 3:16; 2 Peter 1:19–21).

2. The precious Blood (Col. 1:14; Heb. 9:22; 1 Peter 1:18–19; 1 John 1:7).

3. The inliving Christ (John 14:16–17; Rom. 8:11; Gal. 2:20; Eph. 3:17).

4. The blessed Hope (John 14:3; 1 Thess. 4:16–17; Titus 2:13; 1 John 3:1–3).

C. C. Maple

LIKE HIM

1 John 3:2

I. An Assertion—"We know."

A. Many things we do not know: How a soul can exist separate from a body, how we shall think, communicate, etc.

B. But some things we do know.

II. A Manifestation—"He shall appear."

Our Master was not fully made manifest here below:

A. Glory was veiled in the flesh.

B. His deity was concealed in infirmity.

C. His power was hidden under sorrow and weakness.

D. His riches were buried under poverty and shame—but

E. His reappearing will be in "power and great glory."

III. A Transformation—"Like Him."

A. In body: "Who shall change our vile body, [etc]." (Phil. 3:21); "As we have borne the image of the earthly, [etc]." (1 Cor. 15:49). A body sinless, incorruptible, painless, beautiful, etc.

B. In soul: perfect, holy, taught, developed, active, free from temptation, conflict, suffering.

C. In dignity: Kings, Priests, Conquerors, Judges, Sons of God.

D. How this transformation is brought about:

   1. By the mighty power of God.
   2. By the mighty truth of God.
   3. By the Holy Spirit.
   4. By beholding His glory (2 Cor. 3:18).

See Him as He is, not as He was by reflection—partially, dimly, distantly, abased, tempted, despised, mocked, scourged, crucified—but admired, exalted, crowned, glorified,

IV. A Consummation —"When he shall appear."

A. The first stage of this change is regeneration—"He that hath begun a good work in you, [etc]."

B. The last—at His coming (Rom. 8:18–24; 1 Thess. 4:14–18).

V. An Identification—"We."

Not all men—not all professors

A. Those who are born again—"now are we the sons of God."
B. Those who have this hope in them.
C. Those who suffer with Him.

Frederich Rader

"QUICKLY"

Four times does this startling word *quickly* ring out from the book of Revelation upon the dark centuries of probationary time—as if to move us to diligence in duty, vigilance in danger, patience under seeming delay, and to show the great love of the Bridegroom's heart—which will not permit Him to defer the holy nuptials beyond what is absolutely necessary, He is coming as expeditiously as possible. Listen to His voice:

1. "Behold, I come quickly: hold that fast which thou hast, that no man take thy crown" (3:11).

2. "Behold, I come quickly: blessed is he that keepeth the sayings of the prophecy of this book" (22:7).

3. "Behold, I come quickly; and my reward is with me, to give every man according as his work shall be" (22:12).

4. "He that testifieth these things saith, Surely I come quickly" (22:20).

Let not the dust of worldliness clog your ears, nor the din of business prevent you from daily hearing that earnest, arousing word, *quickly.*

J. M. Orrock

THE SAINTS AND THE SECOND COMING OF CHRIST

1 John 3:2

1. They Shall Be Preserved.

"Being confident of this very thing, that he which hath begun a good work in you will perform it until the day of Jesus Christ" (Phil. 1:6; see 2 Tim. 4:18; 1 Peter 1:5; Jude 24).

2. They Shall Not Be Ashamed.

"And now, little children, abide in him; that, when he shall appear, we may have confidence, and not be ashamed before him at his coming" (1 John 2:28).

3. They Shall Be Blameless.

"Waiting for the coming of our Lord Jesus Christ: who shall also confirm you unto the end, that ye may be blameless in the day of our Lord Jesus Christ" (1 Cor. 1:7–8; see 1 Thess. 3:13; 5:23).

4. They Shall Be Like Him.

"Beloved, now are we the sons of God, and it doth not yet appear what we shall be: but we know that, when he shall appear, we shall be like him" (1 John 3:2; see Phil. 3:20–21).

5. They Shall Appear with Him in Glory.

"When Christ, who is our life, shall appear, then shall ye also appear with him in glory" (Col. 3:4).

6. They Shall Receive a Crown of Glory.

"Henceforth there is laid up for me a crown of righteousness, which the Lord, the righteous judge, shall give me at that day: and not to me only, but unto all them also that love his appearing" (2 Tim. 4:8; see 1 Peter 5:4).

7. They Shall Reign with Him.

"If we suffer, we shall also reign with him" (2 Tim. 2:12; see Dan. 7:27; Rev. 5:10; 20:6; 22:5).

Wm. Schweinfurth

"BEHOLD THE MAN"

John 19:5

1. **Behold Him in prophecy (Acts 3:22).**
   The prophets announced His coming (John 1:45; Acts 7:37).

2. **Behold Him in types and shadows** (John 3:14–15).
   First the type and now we see the antitype (1 Cor. 10:11; 1 Peter 1:10–12).

3. **Behold Him in His humble birth** (Matt. 1:21–23).
   It was all according to prophecy (Luke 1:30–33; John 1:46).

4. **Behold Him in His life and teaching** (John 7:46).
   Life without fault. They marvel at His teaching (Matt. 7:28–29; Luke 4:22).

5. **Behold Him in His mighty works** (John 3:2).
   The works—His credentials. No other did what He did (John 10:25; Acts 2:22).

6. **Behold Him in His death and resurrection** (Matt. 27:54).
   By His death He preached as He fulfilled prophecy (Acts 9:5; 1 Cor. 15:1–4).

7. **Behold Him in His coming and kingdom** (Rev. 1:7).
   Born as a lowly babe—returns to sit on a throne (Dan. 7:13–14; 1 Tim. 6:14–15).

C. C. Maple

THE INDWELLING CHRIST AND THE ASSURANCE OF HIS RETURN

1. **The Secret of Christ's Life.**
   Paul said: "I live; yet not I, but Christ liveth in me" (Gal. 2:20).

2. **The Power for Progress in Grace.**
   God said: "I will dwell in them, and walk in them" (2 Cor. 6:16).

3. **The Cause of Fruitfulness.**
   Jesus said: "I in you" (John 15:4).

4. **The Illumination to Enlighten.**
   Paul said: "The word of Christ dwell in you" (Col. 3:16).

5. **The Garrison to Keep the Mind.**
   Paul said: "Let the peace of God rule in your hearts" (Col. 3:15).

6. **The Joy to Gladden the Heart.**
   Jesus said: "My joy might remain in you" (John 15:11).

7. **The Hope of Coming Glory.**
   Paul said: "Christ in you, the hope of glory" (Col. 1:27).

F. E. Marsh

Blessed Assurance

Blessed assurance, Jesus is mine! O what a foretaste of glory divine! Heir of salvation, purchase of God, born of His Spirit, washed in His blood.

Perfect submission, perfect delight! Visions of rapture now burst on my sight; angels descending bring from above echoes of mercy, whispers of love.

Perfect submission—all is at rest; I in my Savior am happy and blest, watching and waiting, looking above, filled with His goodness, lost in His love.

This is my story, this is my song, praising my Savior all the day long; this is my story, this is my song, praising my Savior all the day long.

Fanny J. Crosby